D0261171

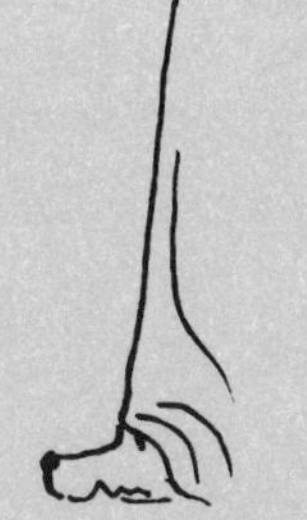

TOTTERING-BY-GENTLY®

TAILS OF TOTTERING HALL

ANNIE TEMPEST

FRANCES LINCOLN LIMITED
PUBLISHERS

Frances Lincoln Limited
4 Torriano Mews
Torriano Avenue
London NW5 2RZ
www.franceslincoln.com

Illustrations archived and compiled by Raymond O'Shea

British Library Cataloguing in Publication Data
A catalogue record for this book is available from the British Library.

ISBN 978-07112-3376-8

Printed in China
Bound for North Pimmshire

9 8 7 6 5 4 3 2 1

Other Tottering-by-Gently books by Annie Tempest:
The Totterings' Diary
Tottering Life (2012)
She Talks Venus He Talks Mars (2011)
In the Garden with the Totterings (2011)
Drinks with the Totterings (2010)
The Tottering-by-Gently Annual (2010)
Out & About with the Totterings (2010)
Available from Frances Lincoln at www.franceslincoln.com

At Home with the Totterings
Tottering-by-Gently Vol III
Available from The Tottering Drawing Room, along with a full range of Tottering-by-Gently licensed product, at The O'Shea Gallery, No. 4 St James's Street, London SW1A 1EF (Telephone +44 (0)1732 866041) or www.tottering.com

Lord Tottering
'Dicky'
Lady Tottering
'Daffy'
Serena
Freddy
Daisy
Gladys Shagpile
HonJon
Scribble
Slobber

2010 © Garlinda Birkbeck

TOTTERING-BY-GENTLY ®
ANNIE TEMPEST

Annie Tempest is one of the top cartoonists working in the UK. This was recognized in 2009 with the Cartoon Art Trust awarding her the Pont Prize for the portrayal of the British Character. Annie's cartoon career began in 1985 with the success of her first book, *How Green Are Your Wellies?* This led to a regular cartoon, 'Westenders' in the *Daily Express*. Soon after, she joined the *Daily Mail* with 'The Yuppies' cartoon strip which ran for more than seven years and for which, in 1989, she was awarded 'Strip Cartoonist of the Year'. Since 1993 Annie Tempest has been charting the life of Daffy and Dicky Tottering in Tottering-by-Gently – the phenomenally successful weekly strip cartoon in *Country Life*.

Daffy Tottering is a woman of a certain age who has been taken into the hearts of people all over the world. She reflects the problems facing women in their everyday life and is completely at one with herself, while reflecting on the intergenerational tensions and the differing perspectives of men and women, as well as dieting, ageing, gardening, fashion, food, field sports, convention and much more.

Daffy and her husband Dicky live in the fading grandeur of Tottering Hall, their stately home in the fictional county of North Pimmshire, with their extended family: son and heir Hon John, daughter Serena, and grandchildren, Freddy and Daisy. The daily, Mrs Shagpile, and love of Dicky's life, Slobber, his black Labrador, and the latest addition to the family, Scribble, Daisy's working Cocker Spaniel, also make regular appearances.

Annie Tempest was born in Zambia in 1959. She has a huge international following and has had eighteen one-woman shows, from Mexico to Mayfair. Her work is now syndicated from New York to Dubai. She has had many collections of her cartoons published. *Tails of Tottering Hall* is the latest and is part of a series of collections around a particular theme.

THE O'SHEA GALLERY

Raymond O'Shea of The O'Shea Gallery was originally one of London's leading antiquarian print and map dealers. Historically, antiquarian galleries sponsored and promoted contemporary artists who they felt complemented their recognized areas of specialization. It was in this tradition that O'Shea first contacted *Country Life* magazine to see if Annie Tempest would like to be represented and sponsored by his gallery. In 1995 Raymond was appointed agent for Annie Tempest's originals and publisher of her books. Raymond is responsible for creating an archive of all of Annie's cartoons.

In 2003, the antiquarian side of his business was put on hold and the St. James's Street premises were finally converted to The Tottering Drawing Room at The O'Shea Gallery. It is now the flagship of a worldwide operation that syndicates and licenses illustrated books, prints, stationery, champagne, jigsaws, greetings cards, ties and much more. It has even launched its own fashion range of tweeds and shooting accessories under the label Gently Ltd.

The Tottering Drawing Room at The O'Shea Gallery is a wonderful location which is now available for corporate events of 45–125 people and is regularly used for private dinner parties catering for up to 14 people. Adjacent to St. James's Palace, the gallery lies between two famous 18th century shops: Berry Bros. & Rudd, the wine merchants and Locks, the hatters. Accessed through French doors at the rear of the gallery lies Pickering Place – not only the smallest public square in Great Britain, with original gas lighting, but it was also where the last duel in England was fought. A plaque on the wall, erected by the Anglo-Texan Society, indicates that from 1842–45 a building here was occupied by the Legation from the Republic of Texas to the Court of St. James.

Raymond O'Shea and Annie Tempest are delighted to be able to extend Tottering fans a warm welcome in the heart of historic St. James's where all the original Tottering watercolours can be seen along side a full product and print range.

Only a labrador can bring an English man to his knees...

WOODNUTT

INTRODUCTION

Tails of Tottering Hall is not only a brilliant book; it is also an unusual book. As the pages are turned it is possible to smell dogs and hear dogs – what they have eaten, rolled in and left on the carpet all become part of reality. How does Annie Tempest achieve this with a paintbrush? The answer is obviously 'quite easily'.

I have nearly always had dogs although when I married Lulu I was briefly dogless – dog anno-domino. Lulu quickly put a stop to that and now we have a black Labrador, almost as bad as Slobber, and a lurcher. Yes, just like Dicky and Daffy we have been there and done that. Why does our lurcher, Briar, always choose to cock his leg against people wearing suits or new green wellies? And how does Reuben the black Lab manage to sneak off and find so many truly repulsive and offensive substances to roll in, before offering a kiss to an unsuspecting Lulu? Then of course with the skill of an exocet missile they will both rush up the stairs and launch themselves on sleeping Lulu if I am up early and forget to close the bedroom door. But despite all of this we love them and in my view a muddy footprint on a new summer dress adds to the feeling of proper country living.

Dogs are companions, friends and workmates. When they are good, we adore them. When they are bad we forgive them. And when they actually return to us and sit, on hearing a command or whistle we are so proud of them.

Annie Tempest catches every mood and as I drift with Lulu towards the state of Dicky and Daffy *Tails of Tottering Hall* will always be close at hand – to throw at Briar when he steals my armchair.

Robin Page

2012 © Martin Carter

Black labrador hairs all over my pillow again...
For heavens sake, Dicky! Sometimes I wish you were more like other men...
...and took a blonde mistress instead...

When it's good to be the third person in a marriage...

Darling – I think he's trying to tell you something ...
Annie Tempest © 2007

It's such a beautiful frosty morning - let's go straight out for a walk, Slobber...
...pyjamas, Barbour, head square, wellies...
...eat your heart out Vivienne Westwood...
ANNIE TEMPEST © 1999

Excuse me, young man! You're supposed to pick up any mess your dog leaves in a London park...
Haven't you brought a plastic bag with you?
No. I'll send a bike for it...
ANNE TENNEST © 1998

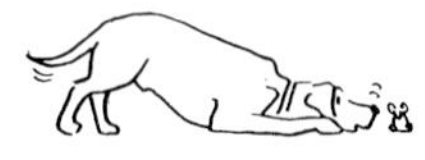

THE FEMALE CHARACTER: An intuition that her guess is more accurate than her husband's certainty...

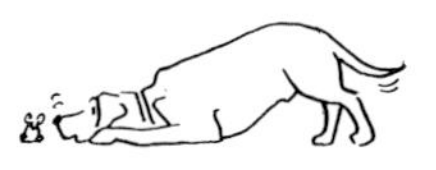

Ah! Slobber - that'll be Dicky back from his trip...
Welcome home, darling!

Uh!Oh! He forgot to bring her a present as well...

"They wouldnt be enjoying themselves so much if they knew that Dotty Dowager's pug ate six pieces of sky this morning..."

Whilst Dicky dines out at the Club, Daffy dines in...

A Good Nose...

A Good Nose...

"The dog has no ambition,
no self interest,
no desire for vengeance,
no fear other than
that of displeasing..."
No wonder they're our best friends...
Annie Tempest
© 2009

What's our climate like?..
You haven't been to England for a long time, have you!
We don't have a climate any more – we just have weather...
ANNIE TEMPEST © 2000

THE TEENAGE CHARACTER: Inability to muster enthusiasm for anything involving being upright and out of doors...

Look at that, Daffy! It's a stunning, crisp and sunny day...
ICE AGE COMING!
TV & RADIO
come on, old girl...
...let's go out and shoot something...
RAM RAIDERS IN ROTTINGBEAN!
NEW SCOUTS HUT HIT BY ARSON
1st SAND DROPS SIGHTED
10% OFF ALL BULBS

Welly, Harry Potter tape, shooting stick, Daisy's sock, mug...
I don't know why everybody else's clutter is so deeply irritating, Slobber...
I mean my clutter is always in exactly the right spot...
ANNIE TEMPEST © 2002

Urgh! I can't take late nights any more. I must give up smoking and drinking...
... my mouth feels like the bottom of an old roasting tin...
Really? Mine feels more like the inner tube of a 1932 Morgan...
ANNIE TEMPEST©2002

Ssitt!.. Stay!!!
What on EARTH are you doing in there, Daffy?
...I'm trying to train my hair but it just won't do as it's told...
Anne Tenfort © 2003

The entire Georgian Society tour trips over an 'avoidable hazard'... Slobber snoozing on the top step...

MARS AND VENUS – A RELAXING EVENING AT HOME...
DAILY MAIL
ANNIE TEMPEST © 2002

THE SPANIEL

This is my private swimming pool...
It's called a cattle trough –
But every time I take a dip
... I seem to get told off...
Poem by Pam Ayres

Lady Tottering

" Shall we stick another dog on the bed - I'm still freezing..."

" I dont think the bed scenes are very realistic..."

I like the Provençal lawn irrigation system...

There's an American dietician giving a talk to the Tottering-by-Gently W.I. this evening, Dicky.
So I see, Daffy – "Food as a means of inter-species communication."...
FLOUR
Perhaps I could persuade him to have a quiet stomach-to-stomach with Slobber afterwards...

Don't worry, Slobber – I've sent out change of kennel cards to all your best friends...

ENJOYING ONE'S HUSBAND'S HOBBIES...

Never too old to... play Pooh-sticks...

THE ART OF ELICITING A CHARITY DONATION...

"I'll beg and wag my tail – you try to look cute..."

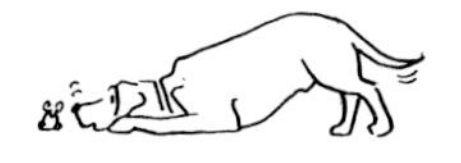

Very original planting on this side. Is it some new look you saw at Chelsea Flower Show?
No that's my grandaughter's idea. She's delegated the design to her working Cocker...
... every time he digs a hole, she puts a plant in it...

Don't you feel sorry for dogs, seeing only in black and white, Lord Tottering?...
Not really...
...faced with that ice green, turquoise and lurid orange dress, I'd count my blessings..
1995 © ANNIE TEMPEST

THE 'TOASTER SHY' GUN DOG...

Annie Tempest©2010

I don't know about Spaniels, Slobber...
they're so highly strung and they have very poor manners...
Look at that! Doesn't he know it's rude to point...

Granny! Why is there an episode of Emmerdale in the middle of our Star Wars video?
Oh no! Slobber! Don't tell me ...
...you sat on the remote while Granny was searching for a blank cassette, didnt you!...

Sally fforth-Wright and her pug view the gun-dog obedience class at the North Pimmshire Game Fair...

"I'm afraid it's just a characteristic of the breed– let them off the leash for two minutes and they run away to their club and drink too much..."

"Darling - it's Hello! magazine on the phone - they'd like to photograph us in our gracious home..."

"... Maybe youd like a glass of water before you go?..."

Living it up!

Don't be scared, Scribble - that's just the noise grandparents make when they watch television...
ZZZZzzzz
ZZZZzzz
Anne Tempest © 2006

"What do you reckon?
Does that
mean
you . . . or me? . . .

TRUE LOVE...

" don't worry; Woofy's only marking out his territory..."

A really special Queen Anne walnut settee, is it? Well, it's not half as comfy as an old towel in a basket, if you ask me...

I gave up smoking on New Year's Eve, actually...
ANNIE TEMPEST©2000
I just tend to light the odd one...
...just in case one of the dogs gets a tick...

Sorry, Daffy... afraid I've just dropped my breakfast on the dining room carpet...
Oh! Don't worry, Iris - I'll bring the cordless hoover...
Come on, Slobber - go seek the dindins...
ANNIE TEMPEST © 2002

He could have been a first-rate gundog but he was terribly abused as a puppy...
How dreadful. What happened to him?
His previous owner used to make him retrieve her fluffy pink slippers...
Good Lord!
ANNIE TEMPEST©1997

I've just sprayed the red drawing room with my air freshener - how does it smell to you, Madam?
Let me see, Mrs Shagpile...
Lavender and lemon on top... with a hint of wet labrador and dry-rot at the bottom...
ANNIE TEMPEST © 1998

Oh hell! Your dog's got into my larder!...
Fiddlesticks, Daffy!
Your larder's got into my dog.
1996 © ANNIE TEMPEST.

The Bracegirdles have had that dreadful dog immortalised in paint, stone, copper, marble...
...there can't be many mediums left...
...I don't know - box?.. Privet?... Jelly?...
TESCO
1995 © ANNIE TEMPEST

He's just started bottom shuffling, Lord Tottering...
When Slobber does that it usually means he has worms...
Annie Tempest ©2009

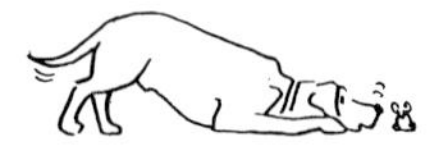

I'm so sorry, lady Reticule-Swype! Mummy just ran your pug over in the drive...
Oh! Tell Daffy not to worry, Serena...
Barnaby was stuffed and due for re-upholstering anyhow...

There comes a time, Daffy, when we all have to succumb to vary-focals...

How on earth do all these mail order catalogues find people prepared to pay for all these strange things?..
Who on EARTH would want them? A giant electric lint-shaver?.. A desk-top sundial?.. A pair of reflexology socks... a light aluminium wheelchair-cum-roof ladder in a bag...
Ooh! A handy pocket-sized microfibre dog towel... I definitely need one of those...
Annie Tempest ©2008

THE LABRADOR CHARACTER : Always at his master's heel...
Annie Tempest ©2005

YOUCH! I've practically sliced my finger off!
It won't stop bleeding - you might have to drive me up to the hospital, Dicky...
PESTO
I wouldn't risk it - it'll be safer to get Slobber to lick it clean...
FILTHY NHS HOSPITALS... MRSA...
Annie Tempest ©2009

This is Slobber – He's our head of security as neither of us can work out how to operate the new burglar alarm system...
Be careful – if you go downstairs in the middle of the night he's liable to give you a nasty lick...
Annie Tempest © 2010

The collar's too tight on your dog, Dicky...
I don't think it is, Grizelda...
Maybe your fingers are too fat...

...

...and that's my grandfather, General Sir Napier Stenchbrook with his beloved dog, Purdey..
...he was rewarded for exceptional performance in the field...
Who? The spaniel or the soldier?
1995 ©ANNIE TEMPEST

Oh! That's GROSS! Scribble's eating a frog! Granny! Stop him!
Annie Tempest © 2008
He probably just likes French food, Daisy...
...it's his little 'amuse bouche' before his din-dins...

You've put on weight, Slobber!
But don't worry - I forgive you...
Imitation is the sincerest form of flattery...
Annie Tempest ©2006

THE MALE CHARACTER: A tendency to lay down the law...
...and then accept amendments...
Annie Tempest © 2007

Look what I've bought for Simon and Claire's wedding present...
We can't give cactuses as a wedding present!
BASC joins ColdCare Gin
They were on their list - apparently they're brilliant for keeping the dogs off the sofas...
Annie Tempest © 2009

THE LABRADOR CHARACTER: A strong drive to please its master...
"Quick! Jump up here - you're getting muddy paws all over the carpet..."

You spoil that dog, Aunt Marigold...
Nonsense, Daffy! He'd get depressed if he thought he couldn't still chase his ball-ee...

Slobber looks very good for his age doesn't he...
Yes - well he gets plenty of exercise, a good diet and alot of love...
...and black felt tip pen on his grey muzzle takes years off him...
Annie Tempest©2010

Aren't you going to stop him chewing up your post, Dicky?!
Certainly not...
... he's my junk mail filter...

Slobber! Scribble! Stop that!
SLOBBER
SCRIBBL
Oh! Leave them alone, Dicky!..
That's my pre-wash cycle...
SLOBBER
SCRIBBLE

QUERCUS AMORATII
Annie Tempest ©2007

TRUE LOVE...

'To retain freshness, biscuits should be kept in an air-tight container...'
I dont think I've got any Tupperware left...
I'd say my stomach is an air tight container, wouldn't you, Slobber ...
Annie Tempest © 2004

ANNIE TEMPEST © 2001

THE FEMALE CHARACTER: A talent for multitasking even when at rest...
Annie Tempest ©2005

My son has invited me out there but I can't go, you see, because of my dogs..
Then he says - 'who's more important - the dogs or your own grandchildren?'...
I hope you told him....
ANNIE TEMPEST

THE FEMALE CHARACTER: A *hoarding instinct*...

"Dicky! You can't possibly throw out my paper bag full of all our dog's baby teeth..."

Do you remember? That was taken on his first birthday...
Ah! There he is on his first day at boarding school...
and look! That was his first retrieve!..
Annie Tempest ©2009

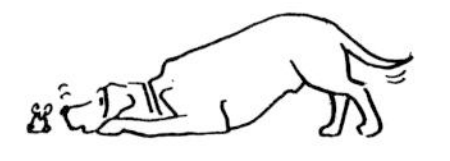

Who on earth's calling Serena at this time of night?...
It's the nanny...
Good God! I hope the dogs are all right!...

So sorry we're late. Bill had to make an important call to the U.S...
Not a business crisis, I hope?
No, no. Just saying goodnight to my dogs at home in Connecticut...
Annie Tempest ©

Slobber Tottering to see the vet...
HAVE YOU GOT FLEAS?
VETERINARY S
PARVO BOOSTERS DUE
And where is he?
HAVE YOU GOT FLEAS?
VETERINARY SU
PARVO BOOSTERS DUE
FRESH BREATH
CANINE DENTAL FLOSS
Damn! I knew I'd forgotten something!
HAVE YOU GOT FLEAS?
VETERINARY SU
PARVO BOOSTERS DUE
CANINE DENTAL FLOSS
Annie Tempest © 2005

I'm glad he's healthy. Would you have any idea what the life expectancy of a labrador is?
Yes. About ten to twelve years. Why?
I was wondering when I could plan a holiday...
DOOM! TM for fleas, worms + ticks!
2010 © Annie Tempest

You have to admit that Labradors have beautiful manners, Daffy...
When they've done something wrong, they always come over and apologise...
Yes, dear - and then do exactly the same thing again...
Annie Tempest ©2011

AAGHRUF
GRROWF
GRR!
GRR
RR!
GR
RR
GRUNAR
ARF GRR
GRR
RRGH!
All you have to do is speak their language...

Guilty as charged...

Labrador Brownie points...
ANNIE TEMPEST © 2001

For the sake of the dogs, the British prefer not to raise their voices in anger...

My goodness! 690,480 single women between the ages of 25 and 44! You see, in our day we weren't into careers like you lot when we left school...
Daily Mail
POPE ELOPES!
We focussed on finding a partner in life... someone to share the ups and downs, one's joys and sorrows, trials and tribulations... someone to love...
Yup. And this generation has cottoned on to the fact that you can have all that from a labrador AND have a career...

That's my dog! He's called Scribble and he's a working Cocker Spaniel...
What's a 'working' Cocker Spaniel? Does he have a job?
Yes. He's Granny Tottering's personal trainer...

For heavens sake! Slobber needs a walk whether it's raining or not - it's not too much to ask when I'm rushed off my feet, is it?..
The way you go on you'd think I did absolutely nothing for you - nag, nag, nag... I'll do the bins and walk the dog in my own time...
Don't interrupt, Daisy - we're having an adult conversation...

ANNIE·TEMPEST©2002

WALKIES
HEELEYS

I'd like a glass of cold champagne and a plate of Blinis, please...
What are you looking at me like that for?..
... a woman's allowed to fantasise once in a while...
Annie Tempest © 2005

Lost her handbag... forgot to kiss the dog goodbye... five past eight...
...got to quickly ring so-and-so... left her lipstick upstairs...
ANNIE TEMPEST © 2003

Annie Tempest ©2006

The blood lines on both sides are impeccable, Dicky...
very even temperament, bright eyes... intelligent ... good hips...
are we discussing dogs or daughters-in-law?...

I gather you need a really good sense of humour to take a Spaniel out shooting with you..
No. Not at all... Heel, boy!!
... but your host does...
Annie Tempest © 2011

Look what I found in that last wood, Lord Tottering – Chanterelles, I think...
Annie Tempest ©2010
Oh! My goodness, Corky! Look at the colour of them! They look poisonous...
Just make sure you try them yourself before feeding them to the dogs...

Awfully sorry to hear that you and Lucinda are splitting up...
Yes. Messy business-we're having a ghastly court battle over custody...
But you don't have any kids!
No. I'm fighting for custody of the labrador during the shooting season...

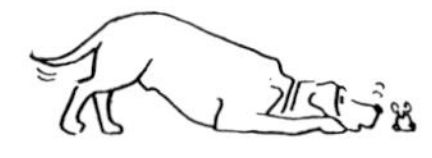

The important business of warming the armchairs before the shooting party's return...
ANNIE TEMPEST © 1999

Christmas Spices
Happy Christmas
Joyeux Noël!
Yuletide Greeting

I think I got away with it...

TOTTERING BRAND

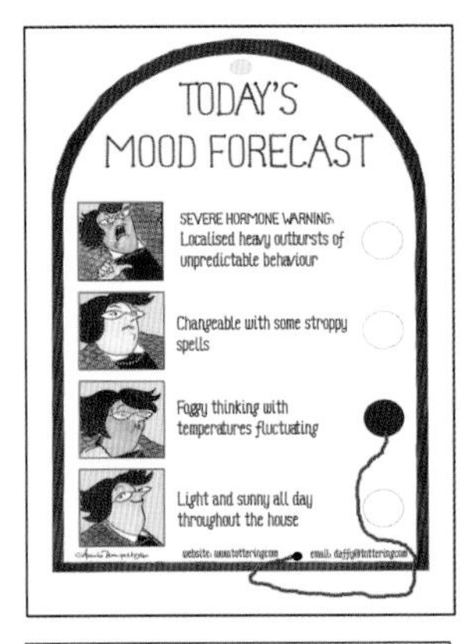

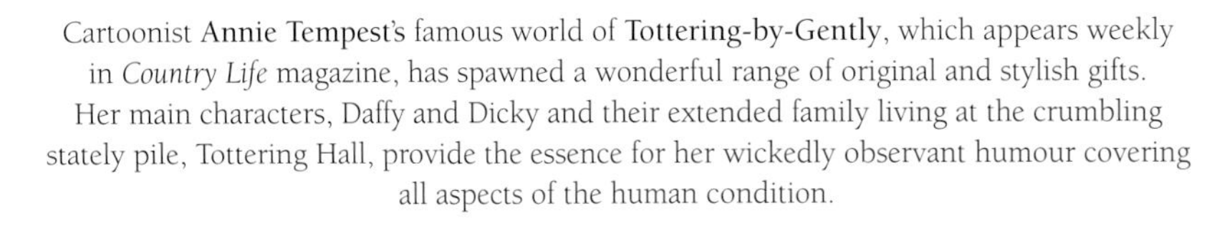

Cartoonist **Annie Tempest's** famous world of **Tottering-by-Gently**, which appears weekly in *Country Life* magazine, has spawned a wonderful range of original and stylish gifts. Her main characters, Daffy and Dicky and their extended family living at the crumbling stately pile, Tottering Hall, provide the essence for her wickedly observant humour covering all aspects of the human condition.

The Tottering range of gifts is suitable for everyone with a sense of fun. Gifts include: a large range of Signed Numbered Edition Prints, as well as digital prints On Demand (any Annie Tempest image produced as a print), books, diaries, greeting cards, postcards, tablemats, coasters, trays, noteblocks, mugs, tins, tea towels, hob covers and much more – we even have our own brand of Tottering-by-Gently Champagne . . .

You can order from our secure website at www.tottering.com or pop into our London shop: The Tottering Drawing Room at The O'Shea Gallery, at No.4, St. James's Street, SW1A 1EF, where all original artwork is available to buy.

www.tottering.com